Multiplication 2nd Grade Math Essentials

Children's Arithmetic Books

Speedy Publishing LLC
40 E. Main St. #1156
Newark, DE 19711
www.speedypublishing.com

Exercise Number: 1

Name: ________________________________ Score: ____

Show your solutions in the space provided.

1. $2 \times 4 =$ ______

4. $11 \times 2 =$ ______

2. $5 \times 10 =$ ______

5. $5 \times 8 =$ ______

3. $8 \times 4 =$ ______

6. $7 \times 5 =$ ______

Exercise Number: 2

Name: ______________________ Score: ____

Show your solutions in the space provided.

1. 2 × 8 = ______

4. 4 × 9 = ______

2. 1 × 3 = ______

5. 4 × 2 = ______

3. 1 × 5 = ______

6. 10 × 4 = ______

Exercise Number: 3

Name: ______________________________ Score: ____

Show your solutions in the space provided.

1. $9 \times 4 =$ ______

2. $12 \times 5 =$ ______

3. $5 \times 9 =$ ______

4. $4 \times 10 =$ ______

5. $3 \times 10 =$ ______

6. $6 \times 3 =$ ______

Exercise Number: 4

Name: ______________________________ Score: ____

Show your solutions in the space provided.

1. 5 × 7 = ______

4. 10 × 5 = ______

2. 5 × 2 = ______

5. 6 × 5 = ______

3. 5 × 3 = ______

6. 3 × 7 = ______

Exercise Number: 5

Name: ______________________________ Score: ____

Show your solutions in the space provided.

1. $9 \times 4 =$ ______

2. $10 \times 4 =$ ______

3. $1 \times 2 =$ ______

4. $3 \times 12 =$ ______

5. $5 \times 12 =$ ______

6. $8 \times 4 =$ ______

Exercise Number: 6

Name: ______________________________ Score: ____

Show your solutions in the space provided.

1. $9 \times 3 =$ ______

2. $5 \times 4 =$ ______

3. $4 \times 4 =$ ______

4. $4 \times 3 =$ ______

5. $3 \times 3 =$ ______

6. $2 \times 10 =$ ______

Exercise Number: 7

Name: ______________________ Score: ____

Show your solutions in the space provided.

1. 4 × 7 = ______

4. 4 × 5 = ______

2. 3 × 1 = ______

5. 3 × 3 = ______

3. 8 × 3 = ______

6. 5 × 3 = ______

Exercise Number: 8

Name: ______________________ Score: ____

Show your solutions in the space provided.

1. 4 × 11 = ______

2. 3 × 9 = ______

3. 11 × 2 = ______

4. 4 × 10 = ______

5. 4 × 2 = ______

6. 5 × 1 = ______

Exercise Number: 9

Name: ______________________ Score: ____

Show your solutions in the space provided.

1. $3 \times 12 =$ ______

2. $2 \times 1 =$ ______

3. $2 \times 4 =$ ______

4. $5 \times 9 =$ ______

5. $2 \times 7 =$ ______

6. $9 \times 4 =$ ______

Exercise Number: 10

Name: ______________________________ Score: ____

Show your solutions in the space provided.

1. $12 \times 3 =$ ______

2. $3 \times 6 =$ ______

3. $5 \times 5 =$ ______

4. $12 \times 2 =$ ______

5. $10 \times 4 =$ ______

6. $5 \times 8 =$ ______

Exercise Number: 11

Name: ______________________________ Score: ____

Show your solutions in the space provided.

1. 4 × 7 = ______

4. 4 × 9 = ______

2. 12 × 4 = ______

5. 4 × 3 = ______

3. 3 × 9 = ______

6. 3 × 8 = ______

Exercise Number: 12

Name: ______________________________ Score: ____

Show your solutions in the space provided.

1. $12 \times 3 =$ ______

4. $4 \times 4 =$ ______

2. $3 \times 3 =$ ______

5. $5 \times 1 =$ ______

3. $4 \times 10 =$ ______

6. $4 \times 5 =$ ______

Exercise Number: 13

Name: ______________________________ Score: ____

Show your solutions in the space provided.

1. $4 \times 8 =$ ______

2. $7 \times 5 =$ ______

3. $3 \times 10 =$ ______

4. $10 \times 2 =$ ______

5. $4 \times 12 =$ ______

6. $3 \times 1 =$ ______

Exercise Number: 14

Name: ______________________________ Score: ____

Show your solutions in the space provided.

1. $3 \times 6 =$ ______

2. $2 \times 5 =$ ______

3. $9 \times 2 =$ ______

4. $5 \times 4 =$ ______

5. $2 \times 2 =$ ______

6. $3 \times 10 =$ ______

Exercise Number: 15

Name: ______________________________ Score: ____

Show your solutions in the space provided.

1. $4 \times 5 =$ ______

2. $5 \times 8 =$ ______

3. $10 \times 4 =$ ______

4. $4 \times 4 =$ ______

5. $2 \times 7 =$ ______

6. $3 \times 2 =$ ______

Exercise Number: 16

Name: ______________________________ Score: ____

Show your solutions in the space provided.

1. $7 \times 2 =$ ______

2. $6 \times 5 =$ ______

3. $10 \times 5 =$ ______

4. $2 \times 11 =$ ______

5. $3 \times 11 =$ ______

6. $8 \times 3 =$ ______

Exercise Number: 17

Name: ______________________________ Score: ____

Show your solutions in the space provided.

1. $2 \times 5 =$ ______

4. $2 \times 4 =$ ______

2. $10 \times 2 =$ ______

5. $11 \times 4 =$ ______

3. $3 \times 6 =$ ______

6. $6 \times 3 =$ ______

Exercise Number: 18

Name: ______________________________ Score: ____

Show your solutions in the space provided.

1. 2 × 2 = ______

2. 9 × 5 = ______

3. 3 × 3 = ______

4. 8 × 2 = ______

5. 2 × 1 = ______

6. 1 × 3 = ______

Exercise Number: 19

Name: ______________________________ Score: ____

Show your solutions in the space provided.

1. $2 \times 6 =$ ______

4. $3 \times 4 =$ ______

2. $5 \times 3 =$ ______

5. $8 \times 4 =$ ______

3. $5 \times 8 =$ ______

6. $3 \times 6 =$ ______

Exercise Number: 20

Name: ______________________ Score: ____

Show your solutions in the space provided.

1. $5 \times 11 =$ ______

4. $5 \times 12 =$ ______

2. $12 \times 4 =$ ______

5. $4 \times 6 =$ ______

3. $6 \times 4 =$ ______

6. $8 \times 5 =$ ______

Exercise Number: 21

Name: ______________________________ Score: ____

Show your solutions in the space provided.

1. $2 \times 1 =$ ______

2. $1 \times 4 =$ ______

3. $9 \times 3 =$ ______

4. $2 \times 11 =$ ______

5. $2 \times 3 =$ ______

6. $5 \times 4 =$ ______

Exercise Number: 22

Name: ______________________________ Score: ____

Show your solutions in the space provided.

1. $1 \times 2 =$ ______

2. $8 \times 3 =$ ______

3. $4 \times 1 =$ ______

4. $5 \times 5 =$ ______

5. $2 \times 2 =$ ______

6. $3 \times 3 =$ ______

Exercise Number: 23

Name: ______________________ Score: ____

Show your solutions in the space provided.

1. $4 \times 7 =$ ______

2. $8 \times 4 =$ ______

3. $4 \times 3 =$ ______

4. $4 \times 11 =$ ______

5. $5 \times 3 =$ ______

6. $10 \times 5 =$ ______

Exercise Number: 24

Name: ______________________________ Score: ____

Show your solutions in the space provided.

1. $4 \times 5 =$ ______

2. $5 \times 2 =$ ______

3. $9 \times 5 =$ ______

4. $3 \times 10 =$ ______

5. $3 \times 7 =$ ______

6. $9 \times 2 =$ ______

Exercise Number: 25

Name: ______________________________ Score: ____

Show your solutions in the space provided.

1. $4 \times 12 =$ ______

2. $2 \times 5 =$ ______

3. $4 \times 8 =$ ______

4. $5 \times 11 =$ ______

5. $11 \times 3 =$ ______

6. $3 \times 2 =$ ______

Exercise Number: 26

Name: ______________________________ Score: ____

Show your solutions in the space provided.

1. $5 \times 1 =$ ______

2. $7 \times 2 =$ ______

3. $4 \times 9 =$ ______

4. $5 \times 2 =$ ______

5. $5 \times 5 =$ ______

6. $4 \times 2 =$ ______

Exercise Number: 27

Name: ______________________________ Score: ____

Show your solutions in the space provided.

1. $4 \times 10 =$ ______

4. $2 \times 3 =$ ______

2. $4 \times 6 =$ ______

5. $4 \times 2 =$ ______

3. $1 \times 4 =$ ______

6. $2 \times 3 =$ ______

Exercise Number: 28

Name: ______________________________ Score: ____

Show your solutions in the space provided.

1. $4 \times 7 =$ ______

2. $5 \times 12 =$ ______

3. $2 \times 12 =$ ______

4. $12 \times 4 =$ ______

5. $7 \times 4 =$ ______

6. $3 \times 3 =$ ______

Exercise Number: 29

Name: ______________________________ Score: ____

Show your solutions in the space provided.

1. $2 \times 8 =$ ______

2. $5 \times 9 =$ ______

3. $5 \times 3 =$ ______

4. $2 \times 7 =$ ______

5. $6 \times 4 =$ ______

6. $2 \times 10 =$ ______

Exercise Number: 30

Name: ______________________________ Score: ____

Show your solutions in the space provided.

1. $4 \times 8 =$ ______

4. $9 \times 3 =$ ______

2. $5 \times 11 =$ ______

5. $11 \times 2 =$ ______

3. $12 \times 3 =$ ______

6. $2 \times 6 =$ ______

Exercise Number: 31

Name: ______________________________ Score: ____

Show your solutions in the space provided.

1. $5 \times 10 =$ ______

2. $12 \times 3 =$ ______

3. $2 \times 3 =$ ______

4. $2 \times 7 =$ ______

5. $8 \times 3 =$ ______

6. $4 \times 4 =$ ______

Exercise Number: 32

Name: ______________________ Score: ____

Show your solutions in the space provided.

1. $3 \times 8 =$ ______

4. $3 \times 4 =$ ______

2. $2 \times 5 =$ ______

5. $10 \times 4 =$ ______

3. $2 \times 1 =$ ______

6. $8 \times 2 =$ ______

Exercise Number: 33

Name: ________________________________ Score: ____

Show your solutions in the space provided.

1. $8 \times 5 =$ ______

2. $4 \times 12 =$ ______

3. $2 \times 2 =$ ______

4. $12 \times 5 =$ ______

5. $1 \times 4 =$ ______

6. $5 \times 8 =$ ______

Exercise Number: 34

Name: ______________________________ Score: ____

Show your solutions in the space provided.

1. $5 \times 5 =$ ______

2. $8 \times 4 =$ ______

3. $9 \times 3 =$ ______

4. $5 \times 2 =$ ______

5. $3 \times 4 =$ ______

6. $12 \times 3 =$ ______

Exercise Number: 35

Name: ______________________________ Score: ____

Show your solutions in the space provided.

1. $5 \times 4 =$ ______

4. $3 \times 3 =$ ______

2. $4 \times 2 =$ ______

5. $6 \times 3 =$ ______

3. $4 \times 3 =$ ______

6. $2 \times 12 =$ ______

ANSWERS

1. 8
2. 50
3. 32
4. 22
5. 40
6. 35

1. 36
2. 40
3. 2
4. 36
5. 60
6. 32

1. 36
2. 2
3. 8
4. 45
5. 14
6. 36

1. 32
2. 35
3. 30
4. 20
5. 48
6. 3

1. 10
2. 20
3. 18
4. 8
5. 44
6. 18

1. 16
2. 3
3. 5
4. 36
5. 8
6. 40

1. 27
2. 20
3. 16
4. 12
5. 9
6. 20

1. 36
2. 18
3. 25
4. 24
5. 40
6. 40

1. 18
2. 10
3. 18
4. 20
5. 4
6. 30

1. 4
2. 45
3. 9
4. 16
5. 2
6. 3

1. 36
2. 60
3. 45
4. 40
5. 30
6. 18

1. 28
2. 3
3. 24
4. 20
5. 9
6. 15

1. 28
2. 48
3. 27
4. 36
5. 12
6. 24

1. 20
2. 40
3. 40
4. 16
5. 14
6. 6

1. 12
2. 15
3. 40
4. 12
5. 32
6. 18

1. 35
2. 10
3. 15
4. 50
5. 30
6. 21

1. 44
2. 27
3. 22
4. 40
5. 8
6. 5

1. 36
2. 9
3. 40
4. 16
5. 5
6. 20

1. 14
2. 30
3. 50
4. 22
5. 33
6. 24

1. 55
2. 48
3. 24
4. 60
5. 24
6. 40

ANSWERS

1. 2
2. 4
3. 27
4. 22
5. 6
6. 20

1. 2
2. 24
3. 4
4. 25
5. 4
6. 9

1. 28
2. 32
3. 12
4. 44
5. 15
6. 50

1. 20
2. 10
3. 45
4. 30
5. 21
6. 18

1. 48
2. 10
3. 32
4. 55
5. 33
6. 6

1. 5
2. 14
3. 36
4. 10
5. 25
6. 8

1. 40
2. 24
3. 4
4. 6
5. 8
6. 6

1. 28
2. 60
3. 24
4. 48
5. 28
6. 9

1. 16
2. 45
3. 15
4. 14
5. 24
6. 20

1. 32
2. 55
3. 36
4. 27
5. 22
6. 12

1. 50
2. 36
3. 6
4. 14
5. 24
6. 16

1. 24
2. 10
3. 2
4. 12
5. 40
6. 16

1. 40
2. 48
3. 4
4. 60
5. 4
6. 40

1. 25
2. 32
3. 27
4. 10
5. 12
6. 36

1. 20
2. 8
3. 12
4. 9
5. 18
6. 24

www.ingramcontent.com/pod-product-compliance
Lightning Source LLC
LaVergne TN
LVHW060832170826
845678LV00010B/1965

* 9 7 9 8 8 6 9 4 4 8 6 0 6 *